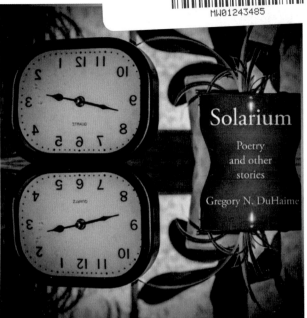

Solarium

Poetry
and other
stories

Gregory N. DuHaime

FIRST EDITION
ISBN: 9798729087686
Imprint: Independently published

Dedication

To my wife and children, thank you for every moment that we have together. To all of my family & friends, I love you. You are ALL my inspiration.

Love, Greg

Love, Dad

*

- *This book is tuned to 444 hz;*

  The frequency of Love . . .

Table of Contents

Introduction

Plates of cheddar popcorn, pretzels and
salted peanuts.
A young boy contemplates the present
moment of his family's life,
after moving back to northern New Jersey.
After reading through dusty books and
tapping the keys of an old organ in the
solarium of his grandparents' home, the
young boy falls asleep.
He dreams of the past, present, and of the
future...

Solarium

Solarium

Two pianos
Played in past time
Growing up watching
Grandfather, sing and rhyme

Lessons on one side
Rhythm sections the latter
A child watching closely
Tick, tap, tip, patter

Although the first
He never got to hear
Many more songs
To dance through his ear

In the solarium
Bronze arms depressed
Salt and charcoal keys
A child tells the rest...

Solarium II

...And dust has found its
home
Along spines of four
angles
Settling within grooves
of cream
A cloth texture beneath
his finger

A door opens, creaking
Heavier steps than mine,
Mold the cherry carpet
beneath
And dust has again,
settled

A deeper voice echoes
But a child cannot
understand
Why must he leave?
Supper time

The red room again
She looks down upon a
table

The color of her eyes,
One may never know

Black, white, glass,
orange
Grace
The knife begins to
carve
Can he go back now?

Sun shines through still
Flakes adrift like snow
A cushion or two brings
comfort
Two more join in,
outside

An organ peering
through,
The window of life
The great tree, an
epicenter
Children find their home

4

She Resigns

Clothes of business black
Laced milk buttoned shirt
A bow tie, steadily waiting
Brunette hair tied back
A tray she balances so finely

Yet she looks down, in thought
A cylindrical glass, gin perhaps
Accompanied by
Essence of orange peel

"Dessert?" She asks kindly.
I respond with, "what is it that you are thinking?"
She is silent.
She writes something down and leaves me waiting, guessing...

Moments later, I am gifted
A dish of fresh vanilla bean iced cream, a finely sliced piece of
homemade carrot cake...

Aunt Patricia beside me,
Sipping her old English black tea; such elegance in her ways.
"Oh, Gregory" she mutters softly...

The lady had returned, and looking me in the eyes she states:
"I want to leave this painting, I resign.

Window Pane

Horizons are
broadened
Through the window
pane
A world ever
changing
Never the same

A man always
moving
From room to room
Through the window
he looks
Depths of life, he will
loom

Stained glass of
beauty
Through the window
again
A reflection is seen
An old wise man, a
friend

Around the bend we
go

And through the
window of time
We are dreaming
again
Into my mind

Perspective is relevant
Beheld in the eye
Man opens window
To bright blue sky

Clouds move softly
Across ocean blue
Just like moving
thoughts
You can see them too

Space and time
Are all that separate
us
Through the window
we see
It is all just, oneness

*

*- And the boy falls
asleep...*

Mother of Science

Dreamer

There he was
In the fungi-fed forest
The dreamer watches
As time passes before him
Horse hair strings,
Brushing lightly
Through his fingers
Rings of tapping, tipping
Slapping, sipping
A voice is carried
Through the wood
Singing a fellow charm
Speaking to us
We must go and follow
A small fire glimmers
Through evening night

A cabin appears
In a clearing
This is his home,
I remember
Two figures appear
Around the fire
Eclectic keys
Sounds of horse hair, again
A djembe, the five-string
Acoustics await our souls
To speak through them
We join hands
With our brothers
And play our hearts away
Until dawn is upon us
We'll meet another day

Alvarez

So bright in tune
A golden wood
Mother of pearl
There you stood

Play through me
Your soul can escape
All notes in time
Tuned to five-twenty-eight (hz)

Oh, hollow body
I hear your cry
Pick me up
Together we'll fly

In a room I sit
With Michael and Victor
Break out the bass guitar,
He'll grab the Schecter

"Play, just play"
Michael had said
It's time to jam
Or just listen instead

He'd grab a CD
Off of the shelf
And share it with us
Open our selves

To possibilities
Of endless notes & chords
Scales on the Alvarez
I'd never be bored

Victor laid down
A steady bass groove
Into a world
Where time never moves

The Warwicker

Deep mahogany
Rich notes of red
Sterling wound
Plucked carefully

Each valley
Stretching shorter
From head
Through body

Cello like
Ensemble sound
Obtuse physique
Nicely round

Golden trestles
Distorted grain
Sound inside my brain
Bass

10

Eight Man

Man, in basement
Eight strings in hand
Play my friend
Show me your land

Dirty blonde hair
Covers his face
Snare drum sits quietly
I'll play the bass

Josh has arrived
He ponders the kit
A kick drum begins
A cymbal is hit

China, crash
Rides, and hats
Snares will snap
Rhymes and raps

Low E's ring out
From Derek's guitar
Bass and drums
Heard near, not far

White gloss body
Pearl inlays
Fretboard trembling
This is jam day

Meet at the basement
He once again said
I'll be right down
How could I forget

As I pluck the bass
To the dirty D jam
J-Rom rocks out
On toms and tams

11

Break time, outside
Cigarettes and cold beer
It's time to talk castles
And band names to hear

We stand there for hours
Overlook the great lake
It's time to call another friend
come on over, Jake

We'll jam "The Flow"
Like good ol' times
Pick up the 7 string
Imma' play some lines

Oh, where is Chris,
When we most need him
That vocal train of his
And super scary grin

We'll shake down Rick's barn
One last good run
All of us together
It's just plain ol' good fun

One more time for good measure
Rhythm sections and phrasing
As we walk the lake roads
Into the stars, gazing

Day Raven

Braids of licorice
Down to toes
A cutting edge
Down the road

The Day Raven
Stops in to play
A sister guitar
Here to stay

Oh, great luthier
Take my sweet Alice
Make her new again
A drink, from chalice

The wine of life flows
From inside your home
Loaves and pastas
And sweet espressos

A room upstairs
Into different worlds
Luthier awaits us
Woods custom burled

Oh, humbled one
Make this anew
Take on a journey
Leave behind a clue

We come together
As one again
Dance in the rain
Or down in the den

It's time for Peasant
From four till eleven
Come back for dinner
Right around seven

The Day Raven
Comes from Taranto
An indigo chariot
Appears at my home

Music, Herself

As I sat with Victor,
Sam and Michael too
We discussed Music
Through and through

It was just theory,
Of course, after all
What I've been shown
The universe, and all

Tools of sound
In my room
New inspiration
Thoughts will bloom

As Uncle Clyde
Picks up the harp
Music so beautiful
Natural, flat, sharp

Moving through all of us
Is the spirit of Music
People love and know
A language so beautifully spoken

"Try easy, my friend, try easy"
Michael - "The Music Lesson"
Victor L. Wooten

- The Spirit of Music Herself

Our Story

Mooney Mountain

Mooney Mountain
Patricia Drive
Rain or sun
Shep will thrive

Up Kurt we go
Then Sue again
We sometimes stop
Here and then

Back again
to 203
Keira, Joe,
Shep, and me

Kristine stops by
Robert as well
He's a fine fellow
His laughter quite swell

Aunt Liz is here
With brownie pie
Her smile so nice
And beautiful eyes

And Nolan laughing
Playing in pool
Sun shining down
Archie's so cool

A grey truck pulls in
Joe is here
With lottery tickets
And lots of cheer!

Time to grill
And say grace again
We're all together
From five til' ten

Shep's outback
Enjoying the spring
Warm weather again
God will bring

Shepherd

Reddish brown coat
Lying in the sun
Absorbing the warmth
Ready for a run

A familiar voice he hears
A jingle of a chain
One ear perks up
Let's beat the rain!

Laces tied tight
Owner ready to go
Shep sees a chipmunk
Oh, oh no!!

He dashes and darts
As quick as can be
Barely holding back
About to break his leash!

Up onto Mooney
We finally get walking
Another dog in distance
Growl, ruff, Barking!

Neighbors we will see

And always wave hello
McCarthy's on her tractor
Planting seeds to grow

We grab her mail
And bring it on up
She pets Shep on the head
"Awe, what a sweet pup"

We move on with our walk
On down past Kurt drive
A walk to the sewer again
Where Shep will always
thrive

Almost back to Joe's
A squirrel runs up a tree
Shep must stop and bark
And have one last pee!

In the house we go
Before the rain storm
comes
Tomorrow is another day
Where Shep will walk and
run

19

Dominican goddess

Silk blonde hair
Waving, against the ocean wind
Selenium air fills our lungs
Purifying our mind and body
We read together.
The shade of a coconut tree,
Guides us
The sun of the Dominican
Warms our souls

A romantic experience with you,
My Goddess
Dressed in pure essence of white
You dance between beach trees
A pear-shaped diamond makes home on your hand
As we love and live, laughter together on the sands

A great sea of love lies before us
Gowned yourself in red beauty
Dining together as sun sets quietly
Tobacco chocolate, Pomegranate gloss of your lips
Johnny Gold joins a glass
And away we sip

And away we go, into the night
You are my beauty,
You are my light
One day we will wed
And bear forth great fruit
Dominican goddess
I love you

Foxy!

Where is he? Where is he?
Where did he go?
Cream sickle colors
Oh no! Oh no!

I'm sure he's just hiding
We'll find him today
A soft little blanket
It's okay, it's okay!

Around all around
Look we must look
Foxes and hounds
Are in every book!

Oh where, oh where
Could foxy be!
In your room?
Or drinking tea?!

Wait!
☐ There he is!
"Foxy!"

Foxy was hiding
Under the bed
Cute and fluffy
Orange and red

A black button-nose
Ears and whiskers
Nobody knows
Shhhh! Whisper!

And away to sleep
Now we must go
With foxy in arms
In winter with snow

Goodnight, goodnight
It's time to dream
Little boy Nilly
Drifting downstream

Winifred Jane

Winifred Jane
On down the lane
A skip and a hop she goes

Chalk on the walk
A lil' hop scotch
And off to play she goes

With friends she plays
On sunny Sundays
And off to church she goes

Winifred Jane
Dancing in rain
And off to sleep she goes

An English muffin
In the morning
And off to school she goes

Make sure it's buttered
Because it's Monday
A skip and a hop she goes

*

Blessed Reconciliation

Box of Pieces

This is Beauty

There, at the table

There sat sixty-four

Side by side

Thirty-two dark, and light, no more

There they stood

An army of sixteen

It is beauty, it is war

Declined

Declined!

Thy Black Monarch stands

Nine points on her crown

Thy diagnolist, moving swiftly

Across darkened spaces

Of burled wood

Encompassed to four corners

Check! She declared

Your little men will fall at my will

For I have captured your castle

Mate

For he was trapped,

Within the six

Escape was no option

She dances downward

From the eighth rank so elegantly. . .

A lone bishop stands beside her

For you my King,

Thy kiss of death

Mate

Across the Desk

He appeared after dusk
At the desk with a book
Reading a passage
And then moving a rook

I ask him a question
And with a subtle reply
He gives me an answer
Which opens my mind

The silent philosopher
I liked to call him
And then he was gone
With slightest of a grin

Come back at five
Another game of life
He looks at me quietly
Maybe, another night

*

The Spirit of Chess, Himself...

Corridors

Corridor

Oh, how many doors
A darkened hall lies before you,
Four floors

A labyrinth in disguise
Two lights, many eyes.
And truth you may seek here,
Only to hear, lies. . .

A shadow follows through
The darkened corridor
With you
A man dressed in blue

Corridor II

Two In the morning
A stable chair by the telephone
In the corner of a darkened room

A man makes his way up a flight of cold
concrete stairs
A usual routine for this time of morning

Thunder, rumbling in the distance, rain
patters the rooftops

A small sound captures his interest
He looks left, into the darkened room
There is no light there, there is no life here

Tables, benches, maybe a deck of cards
Checkers too
A few pieces of left behind clothing, chess
Maybe a shoe

But there is one chair,
Sitting stable, by a telephone
In the corner of the darkened room

Another sound of strange movement,
A lightning flash
Returning to darkness, he shines his light

Was there ever a chair here to begin with?
By the telephone?
He asks himself
Leaving, in quite a hurry . . .

George R. Dunningham

6'1" standing tall

Dark chocolate coat, trench-like

Off-white collared button-down

Deep notes of rosé, cherry tie

Windsor's full knot

Glossy mirror shine

Slacks, creased

Buckle, glistening

Jet matte black, slicked back

Ends of a stache' curled, perfection

Eyes of deep ocean

Today he dresses blue

Reflections

At the Edge

Edge of the continent

Grain beneath me

Body of water

Inside, around me

Watch the blood moon

appear to rise

Reflections of solar winds

Settling at bayside

Sun will set, and soon rise

For it is darkness,

At the edge, of the continent.

Stars come out to play and shine

As we watch space move,

Through Earth's own eyes

Aunt Patricia

Ridgewood, New Jersey
A sea of clover grass
Dandelions dancing wildly
Ivy climbing her home
She rests on her porch quietly
In the afternoon sun
Listening to all things
Olivia street, nearby

Tomato garden growing
A water well
Father leaves on his bicycle
Into town he goes
For coffee, a book,
Nobody knows
Brick paths making way
Cobblestone roads

Back home again,
with Aunt Patricia
3pm, a gong like sound rings
English tea time
Cake, crackers, conversation

Come all who are here

Top of the Mornin'

Good morning, Irish
cream
Espresso roast, latte
dream

Cinnamon swirl,
cocoa dust
Every day, coffee
robust

Rainbow sky, pot of
gold
Little leprechaun, oh
so bold

On my mug, dancing
in cheer
A cup of joe for you,
my dear

To the parade, off we
go

Through the town, see
the show

From Grandma's
house
And Through March
snow

Wild green clover
Watch it grow

Oh, young four leaves
A season of green

Bagpipes sing
And spring it seems

Top of the morning'
And all a good day

A little bit of Irish
Can go a long way!

Conrad's

A smooth white box
Wrapped in cloth green ribbon
Waiting for the children
It's Easter morning again

Grandfather greets us,
"Hello children, good morning"
Such delight and cheer fill the room

We unwrap the box
A large Conrad's chocolate egg
Sits peacefully inside
Children indulge right away

Gold lace ribbon I
A little toy bunny
Jelly beans
An assortment of flavors

The hollow milk chocolate egg
Breaks into several pieces
And we fight over who gets which one

It's Easter morning again,
At our grandparents' home
Off to church we go
Shall we go for a walk after, perhaps?

Carolina Train

Father brings me to the track
To watch the train, go by
We wait patiently as usual
Parked in his car on the side

Quiet, as air stands still
A gray and cloudy setting
Suddenly in the distance
Faint sounds are heard peddling

We exit the car
Ground trembling beneath
Soot and smoke
We'll soon see

Parallel steel bars
Ring with familiar tone
A ghost like whistling approaching, alone

A faint light appears
Through the distant fog
Red lights flashing
Alarms going off

Striped crossing bars drop
At the railway crossing
Heavy, slow
Charcoal engine rumbling

Cargo freight to follow
Oil cars too
Unknown boxes rest steadily
Rusted paint of blue

Flat cars follow
Nearing the end
Here comes the caboose
Around the last bend

There we stand
When train is gone
Into the fog
Singing its song

Until next time
Carolina train
We pack up and leave
As it begins to rain

A penny left on the track, flattened

Olive Tree

Raven in the olive tree
Looking down at me
And as I look back up
Three eyes are all I see

So, I close my eyes
Letting them fill with white
Today I fly with the raven
Off we go, take flight

So many lands away
To the wall we go
Winter is upon us
As we fly through ice and snow

A dragon we seek beyond
In which once was lost
King of the Night has taken him
Returning through the frost

An army marching forward
Giants with them too
A wall torn down
And Broken into two

Horns are sounding as men fall
Down the icy cliffs
Army marches through unscathed
As the season shifts

Winter moving south again
I must warn the others
Return to the olive tree
I tell all my brothers

-   *Thank you, GOT*

Grandmother Gardner

43

October 25th, 2000

Wednesday night
Around Ten o' clock p.m.
Trying to fall asleep in the red room
Restless, reading stories
Characters from trading cards
Mickey Mouse runs around laughing,
In circles above me

Finally, lights out
I close my eyes
Still restless, though
A ten-year-old boys' anticipation of Halloween
night…

Suddenly, I notice something
A chill enters the room
I look up
To see an aura of purple
An elderly woman looking back at me

I ran downstairs to find my mother
She was sorting through old family photographs
I told her what had happened
She tells me,
"Today is the day your grandmother passed away" …

I sit in silence with her

May 9th, 2010

Sunday morning
Mother's Day
About one o' clock a.m.
I lay down in bed for sleep
A restless mind, as usual
Contemplating,
My place in the world
A cold breeze moved past my skin
But, the windows weren't open, I thought

Rolling over to my left,
There she was, again
The glowing purple aura
Of an elderly woman's face
Staring back at me

I jumped up quickly
Hiding on the living room couch
She must have been looking for mother today

I spoke to mother in the morning,
Wishing her a happy Mother's Day
I told her what had happened
She reminded me,
"Today is your grandmothers' birthday" …

I sit in silence with her

45

May 20th, 1990

Sunday morning, again
Approximately two o' clock a.m.
A baby boy is born

A young woman had overheard her talking
during her sleep later that day

"You have a beautiful baby boy"
She had said to herself
Grandmother was speaking through her,
again...
"But she passed away when I was only six
years old",
She had told the woman upon waking...
But the woman had already left the room...

*

"I wish I could have gotten to know you in this world, grandmother…
However, the physical life is only temporary…
For the spiritual life lasts for eternity...

So,
I'll see you up there, one day...

Love, Gregory

After Thoughts

The Read Book

Mint tea is minty
The red book was read
An orange is orange
What's said has been said

It Is Not

It is what it is

And that's all it will ever be.

For if it was something different,

Then it wouldn't have been

What it was in the first place.

For then, it wasn't.

It is not, anything.

But, it was what it was.

Wasn't it?

What was it?

Tomato Days

A tomato on a vine

In the heat of September

Ripening

1443

Those three hands

Tell a story

Freeze them

They tell of a moment

Release them

They are eternity...

My Friend, Cedar

Cedar oak nightstand
Sitting in corner of room
Silently waiting

*

For master to come
Patiently waiting for him
Read a book again

Set, Sail

Ship at sea

Anchor lowered

Bobbing with waves gently

Clouds pass overhead

Like thoughts in mind

Hoist the anchor

And sail with them

Where will the Sea

Take me today

Cliffs

Sometimes life gives you a cliff

You'll either walk away from it

Walk along side of it

Or jump off and fly...

C o l d

What is cold?

Cold is just a reference

It is a perception

Cold is a relevant term

Cold is what you are

When you are not

It is just, an absence

*

Place something else there instead

Silent Tree

Black birds singing

Harmonious tone

Dancing together

In the tree

Love in their hearts, together

Silence comes over them, though

A cousin flying near, for a visit

Conductor of the orchestra

Has arrived

Diverged

And as I stand there
The platform of life envelops me
A quarter lit wood from moon before me
And a whisper in my ear...

Take the one which none have traveled...

It was my friend, Frost,

Again

...and the boy wakes up

Solarium

Gregory N. DuHaime

2021

Made in the USA
Middletown, DE
05 April 2021